THE NINE SENSES

Also by Melissa Kwasny

Reading Novalis in Montana
Thistle
The Archival Birds

I Go to the Ruined Place:
   Contemporary Poems in Defense of Global Human Rights,
   coeditor
Toward the Open Field: Poets on the Art of Poetry, 1800–1950,
   editor

THE NINE SENSES

Melissa Kwasny

milkweed
editions

Published 2011 by Milkweed Editions
Printed in the United States of America
Cover design by Rebecca Lown Design
Interior design by Connie Kuhnz
The text of this book is set in Berstrom.
11 12 13 14 15   5 4 3 2 1
First Edition

Please turn to the back of this book for a list of the sustaining funders of Milkweed Editions.

Library of Congress Cataloging-in-Publication Data

Kwasny, Melissa, 1954–
    The nine senses / Melissa Kwasny. — 1st ed.
        p.   cm.
    ISBN 978-1-57131-437-6 (pbk. : alk. paper) — ISBN 978-1-57131-832-9 (e-book)
    I. Title.
    PS3561.W447N56 2011
    811'.54—dc22

                                                                2010033324

This book is printed on acid-free paper.

for Bryher

Contents

THE NINE SENSES

I.

In recapturing the intentions on which the constitution of this universe depends, in which the Earth is represented, meditated, and encountered in the person of its Angel, we discover that it is much less a matter of answering questions concerning essences ("what is it?") than questions concerning persons ("who is it?" or "to whom does it correspond?") for example, who is the earth? who are the waters, the plants, the mountains? or, to whom do they correspond.

— Henry Corbin

The Language of Flowers

I wish you were here on my arm. I wish I could crawl between your sheets. My Poppy. My Tulip Tree. My Sweet Basil. You are what I used to dream of as a child, what my mother did, not so much a dress as its fabric, pink dotted swiss, a white voile shirt with French cuffs. Tell me your name, what you seek, and to what you aspire. I will mount a campaign for your world. Magnolia, cloudy and thick, each petal the exact temperature of a hand. It is Saturday morning, we are living near lakes, luxuriant, privileged creatures that we are. Our authors say cypress is the favored tree of the earth. Say that flowers are the liturgy of the angels. Wings peeled back so they lift on the breeze. Centered, the golden ovaries bees feast on. Drunk as a young girl on the words of Dylan Thomas, I stagger in the streets of my small town, moonwalking the river, saying sun of our balled fruit, raw honey. I stick my fingers into the champagne flute of a lily. Everything bridal white becomes stained. I can't help but be selfish being faithful to myself. Dabbing it behind the knees. Yes, frosting.

Leaf

Oak stem, rational, its routes laid out like Roman water lines, insect eggs in the pocket of each intersection. Enter the tapestry room where a fire is glowing. Who taught you how green proceeds out of the red? Your life is so different now, healed in a way. Is this the shape of your healing: out from a center stalk, ginkgo's narrow pleats, pressed seams of oak, embossed of maple? They are stretched to their limits. All skin. Yet they breathe the same air you breathe, breath of the wealthy, which is cleaner than most, breath of the poor whom they occupy. Read the palms of the earth in child's pose. You think all you need is to be thin, to be this close to your purpose. Torn with loss. Limp without root. How can you disavow anything's inner life? If all you think about is when you will sleep, what you will read, no wonder the wind lifts without a word. Everything betrays you with its promise. So what is the answer? Oak leaf splayed like the wake of a ship. Your route: straight through the middle.

Sacraments

The green of grass seems personal, ours, because it was there when we were safe, young in our boredom. Cypress, pink scent of flour and water. Water, easy, prolonged. If Walt Whitman were the pilot, I wouldn't be afraid to fly. There would always be swallows and a motor. The vanishing, not the vanished pastoral. Though there is still time to sit at the boathouse. Pond sheen. Fish coin the surface. We don't think of slaves. We don't torture. What we have against the sacramental is that we will avoid it at all cost. Baptism: goose wings beat the surface. What are holy orders without something to obey? Bread of our clay, dropping to our leaves, all the deciduousness we can muster. Light a metropolis over the cleft. Weather is open here, closed like our days. The migrating birds try to stay above us. Confirmation: we are here, though we confess the hours when no one knew where we were. How they followed us into adulthood. Penance we might save for last.

Attar

Night blooming. Suckle of honey. What the mockingbird wears to keep his balance. Hair-thin like the girls here who skip dessert but allow themselves real cream for their coffee. The man who combs his beard while praying, the Sufis say, is not admitted to heaven, though he repents by tearing it out. Silly man, see how he is still obsessed with it. This evening, after dinner, I go walking, the perfume Irene has given me sprayed on my wrists. I start with the trees, more simply with the leaves. I walk my way in, scenting the grasses. Where the country begins: fox left like a dirty rag on the road, folk who handle snakes to heal themselves. Better than drugs and cheaper, Irene said. Everyone has a need for transcendence. William Carlos Williams knew nothing of what it is takes for a woman to stand naked in her own house. Cancer in her bones, dancing to Roy Orbison. No, I won't ever be cured, Irene told the thin girls. It's in the nature of the disease.

Sweetbriar

Today, my cusp. I have hit full bloom. Already you can feel me close,
on my way back to you. You cannot see what rose is at my lips or
where its tender arbors in my hair, white, soft as banana. Today, I am
glutted with gloss. Today, anything I don't like I call postmodern. Go
inside a stone, that would be your way. I am wandering the woodlots
of childhood. No one knew then what to call the hatched vines
snaking up these trunks like a hair shirt. But the pauses I remember,
when the country lane gladdened the shed summer light or when
the brown water disappeared under oak. Oak large as mountains.
It is a wonder any one of us survived. I hid in the lilacs, their
voluptuous violet shade, the cool dirt underneath I would dig my
hands in. My people, or "kind grandparents of the corn and sun"
have all but disappeared from the fields. We had a pact, much like
the one I think I've made with you. Hey, daydream, though the boys
were harsh and cornered us. Though our mothers didn't protect the
girls. We love those girls, would fill our lives with them.

Sanctuary

Under oak. Light that opens like an eyelid to the same trunks, same patch on leaf or leafmeal, then closes. Then opens. The same stuttering pink light. Someone arrives with luggage. Someone has plans to make the best use of her time. And then the time is done. All the eternals—having a father, a mother—are changing form, leaving before I've really understood them. Yes, this is how things happen: one dreams of strawberries, and they are served today for breakfast. One opens a book to the page, "When my father died." I think of him this morning, like a fawn in the long grass. Paralyzed by fear after the diagnosis. (He wanted to speak in tongues. He wanted to travel.) Should I mourn him already, while he is still alive? Oh, Visitor, the silver spoons are clanging in and out of the wind. Above, the periodic tabling of thrush. I could never reach him there. Where reach him now?

Sparrow

The dawns are numbered, as I am. Though I remain ever after in a state of surprise, like a child, dumbfounded by the word "Enter." My name is small, a garden-mint, a sprig to decorate a plate. I rarely try to speak for others, and consider the words I say, not like the mockingbird who repeats banalities, not like the robin, habitual, not like the rabbits who are silent but move loquaciously. Clack of dried pea pods, cloud of mosquitoes, one can have too many roses in the house. The world is loud, anguished by its processes. Though perhaps it is wrong to settle, as I have settled, for the simple meal, the cutting garden, the circumscribed stroll by the pond. When what I want is to sing something monumental. My family is rough. I wish I could smooth them. I have been lucky. Not married out to trash men. But while I sleep, the great winds come. Spruce forest. Pine forest. Fir forest. A door opens. A door slams shut.

Shell

Bluff and double bluff. We could make ourselves sick waiting for this place to open up to us. Polished by our childhoods. Bruises the waves leave. Shell: skinned knee, scraped marble. We know too much about process to try to get around it. What is vital is sometimes hidden inside bone. Bramble of the blackberry that blocks the entrances. As if we weren't meant to be here, though here we are outside, loud-colored to the heron. Morbid, the idea of rubbing through one's own skin, yet we yearn to stick our fingers inside. While the dead make their way through the custom lines. Shell: a quiet verb, slowed by its own sound, gull wings dipping over the clam beds. What if they disappeared, these sculpted, painted things? What would we do without their number, their secret congress? This thinking placed outside ourselves has gotten us here, an interior flame-soft, brushed against a cloud, small cloud of bleeding things, gray feathers.

Bamboo

To be almost dead, that careful. Hollow-boned like the birds. Though one is numerous, part of a pack. To expect less of each other. To glade instead of grove, stand instead of grotto. A tender gardener, one might say, who can twist the trellises. Here is where we make our stand, one might say. A body that breathes will eventually make its own noise. For those trying too hard, here is shade. One could live next to people and know one's presence heals. One could have an empty heart as they do. Bamboo grows straight, marrowless. Look, how we are bent and we have marrow. Down here, the shuffle of leaves barely reaches the still trunks. No matter the words spoken in leaving. Bamboo. It is a child's word one wants to repeat. One wants to continue to wish the other well.

Delight

A spirit that is limited, small as "I imagine," one that flutters on the shoulder between concrete and abstract, a bird's call, not its song, in the distance. It is the fragrance of your voice or the colors in what you say, the floral prints, not the solids. Palms laid out like tables spread, mangos with salt, fried potatoes. It is the feeling you perhaps learned as a child leading your mute twin by the hand, pointing out the yellow-headed blackbirds. Delight you must have learned in order to speak for him. Sweet Heart. Red Clover. Cardinals strung along the fence like paper lanterns. We want to go out in the world no matter what. We want to come back home with plans to plant things. Salutations, oh pigeon! And fireworks for graduation! Pine and fir so we can tell the difference between them. The mind thinks of all the boughs and stars it wants to give, unaware of all that's lost at the periphery. Dear Epicurean. Dear Carnation. Dear Frivolously Blue.

Ophelia among the Flowers

after Odilon Redon

The body is full of cadences. The garden, in fact. A party, by which
I mean candles. Dresses, yes, because it is inside them we want
to be, weighing nothing, hair in our eyes, running up the steps to
meet a lover. One begins with salutation, something all the old
cultures knew. Good night. Good morning. You are a gift to me.
One welcomes the ostracized back into the fold by reciting a list of
their good deeds. An eyelid closed in sleep might hide the color
of this hollyhock, a dark pink silk batiste. Poppy, bright amulet of
the blood. But who are these flowers? My friend has died, is dying,
might die. I sit in the garden under clouds. Long enough to watch
the petals detach in the wind, flutter like fish after touching ground.
O, you must wear your rue with a difference, mild and soiled, like
silk in heat. Baby's breath twisted through my hair.

The School of the Dead, the School of Roots, and the School of Dreams

title after Hélène Cixous

White shoot germinating from the burlap seed, wet, dark, deflated now. What is the earth? Rosary of black beads, clumped. A decade between them. Home of the sorrowful and digestive mysteries. My peas didn't rise. What is under there to maim us, disable us? A sparkle at the deep place as if water pooled there. When I was digging with the spatula, planting the pinks, I struck something hard, skull-like. What is the earth? Bad queen searching for simples in the dark. Cabbage world. Old country. Underlife. While the coffee grounds settle, while the sweetened root tea thins our blood. What is the earth? Our security alarm, our savings. *Please don't talk as if you're going to die.* Silver reeds poking like tent poles through the tarp. Rotting thatch of the summerhouse. What is the earth? Brew pub of purgatory, slop bucket of souls. In a nutshell. Gravy.

Nettle

for Patricia Goedicke

Green clusters of soft beads, the nettle is flowering. When I disappear, you said, write and tell me everything. Snakes slide, when they hear my footsteps, further into the weeds. The tide shudders as it turns over each stone. Is this what it was like as earth began to end? *It started out in loneliness and turned to poetry.* Here: a scribble of seabirds, a peak across the Sound, so distant and vague, like your death to me. Last night, an Iranian doctor performed that tongue-cry she had heard the Arabs use at weddings and funerals. She had examined Fidel Castro and pronounced him fit, four times more charismatic than Clinton. Somehow, I thought you would want to know. Everyone is starting to take on the appearance of ghosts. Rain tips the needles of the cedar. *If our days are the ritual we perform for the dead.* If our days are the ritual we perform for the dead. I wade into the current and leave it open for you. I find excuses to say your name.

The Nightingale's Excuse

Wind, as we walk on the plains. I am crazy about you, that extreme subjectivity. So we duck for the coulees, which is where the cattle go, wearing the ground down between the junipers. Piss-green, to match my peevish mood. Our lives have changed. How is it we didn't notice? We are gray haired, wandering among ruins. The berries in the drylands are pithy and thick. Tin and glass tossed intact into the gullies. Who knows? Perhaps we are at the end of time. Blue aromatics tucked behind our ears. The nightingale's excuse: she is too much in love with the rose. Too fiercely jealous to leave. Are you a plant, a tree, the phlox, the sage? You cannot weigh much less than the moon. I am not used to sharing the green-robed angels on high. But here I am, trusting them with you. Between the wagon trail of the quest and the swell of the new, there is a crowded city pouring through the heart. And the self? Nest constructed of field grass and flower paste. One the masters say we must give up.

II.

Winter Bouquet

Winter bouquet (yellow carnations). Winter Still Life (pomegranate drawn with the figures of a dream). The tiniest fleck of rock the wind tears off. I think of the stars. How can I? A man sets himself on fire to protest the war. A man is tortured inside a prison until he cannot speak. In our curtained days, in our walks along the railroad beds, constructing our alter egos, our additional force. Winter bouquet (rosehips, snowberry, spruce needles). Winter bouquet (oil of fir rubbed into my gloves). A famous Danish artist constructs a crystal sun and people queue up outside the museum to see it. It grieves and buries the heart, a throbbing stone. It lifts the heart, a rose stripped of its petals. What if the morning never comes? Deep shade the winter feeds in, our ministrations too close, tracing flowers, unearthly fruit inside the margins. And doing what, the winds unruly. Here, you say, bringing my gloves to my face, see as if the days will sometime lighten.

Almost Ice

after Morris Graves

We left the house to winter, the book with only a few pages left to read. Most of the important people we had made time for. The snow bedded down like a herd of antelope between the tufts of yellow grass. And along the bank, the water slowed into a kind of lace. *Moth plus.* Almost ice. Barges grind against the pier. A sound with the sound of glass in it. A knife through frosting. What I like, you say, is that a whole beautiful day will disappear, and then part of a day that was not particular will take its place. The pace we keep, walking, light as ghosts. Sun circular and ancient behind a scrim. Like something from a myth, the one where the desert slopes are dug up, and a petrified forest is discovered underneath. *White writing.* The morning is quiet and blurred. The way strangers who love to read talk to each other. When the artist lived in the country, he painted the sounds of the night, inventing the invisible animals from what he heard.

Ground for a New Goddess

title from a painting by Morris Graves

Where the roads cross, facing the water, the drying up of rivers
at our backs. Flowers, tongue-petals, we lick the shore. The light
lapping down. Let there be a turning, let the worst not happen. If
we were born to say goodbye to the earth, as we know it, to wrap
and cleanse the body. If we were born to the intersection, in the
crossing. Smile on this world, old goddess of blue and green. Pain
so deep it rags the seaweed. Puddling as we do in our lonely huts, in
our sewers and low spots where the refuge floats. Afterimage of blue
in the once sky. Almost north. Almost delectation. In the forests to
the east, there were once elm. Over there, where the shorebirds
used to float in a long line. Were they floating over a school of fish
or a warm trough? What does the soul do in its last days? The tyrant
in prison saved the crusts from his bread to feed the birds. We learn
this from his nurse after we hang him. The human soul, I mean, the
one who caused this.

At the Shore

Clouds, all hovering. Yesterday, like a gull's wing. Soft as the tiniest bird eating thistle. Today, slick as a coot. Hissing like asphalt. Cleared of incense. One could write a monograph on the color blue. In *Letters on Cezanne*, Rilke compares the shades of sky to those he found in paintings—blue of Vermeer, blue of the Venetians. Poor poet, weaving his theory of solitude on the loom of Paris rain. Beginning a novel he would never finish. The hills, the cars, the spires recede. Closed with flecked muslin, sometimes flannel. The shoddy Polish blue of the other side of town, someone always whispering behind the curtains. Cinderblock blue. Proletarian blue. Blue rationed to the backstory of history. There's a chill in modern society, Adorno wrote. Clouds the color of a low drone or drake. Cormorant, the impending sky. As if the ferry we need to take to cross the water never arrives. Buck up, little soldier. March on.

The Trumpet Place

after Paul Celan

Say you've been dealt the King Lear. The father with the rotting member. In the home you are not happy in, do you talk to god? Who holds your death as ransom. Who needs his wife. Whose huge hands are now soft as a child's. *Deep in the glowing / text-void,* jamming the stream, you wade in further than the sign advises. While no one relaxes, watching for flaws. What is the opposite of thanksgiving for Father? His resentments, his theatrics of the poor? Poor woman with her plastic bags, picking up litter. "What have I done?" the homeless woman shouts to the sky. To the people who avoid her in the park. Playing the child has always meant saving yourself, swimming to shore and running for dear life. Alone in the house you built, far from the fighting, you indulge the confessional poetry that keeps you young. Waiting for the silence to break with uncalled-for complaint. Waiting for the tests to come back, as you knew they would—negative.

Woman Inside a Tree

after a film by Shirin Neshat

In the Iranian movie, the woman who stands inside the tree
doesn't wake. Like the butterfly, she is dreaming the world, or she
is dreamt by it. Here, sniff her hands. She knows your father. She's
met your mother. From which direction do her half dreams come?
Over the ridge: a village of men in dark shirts and pants. It is not
that she can make them inconsequent. It is not simply a matter of
sleeping. She slips inside herself, as one does, into the folds of the
trunk. Her roots meet blood sacs, hermitages. Chunks of amber.
Oh, crown—she knows the birds, even the large ones. Today, the
announcement. The president is sending more troops. In direct
violation of the peace the people asked for. What can one woman
do, a desert shrine? The camera focuses within the compound, the
courtyard, the stone arcade. There is not enough oil, not enough
water. Even now, the men are breaching the stone wall. Yet, it is
we who are terrorized on her behalf.

The Lights of Earth

after Gina Berriault

We have felt them land, fragile, ornate as venetian glass. Hand in hand—how they broke between the rains. Into a small pond with mallards. A passel of frilly mushrooms. Winter pupa hung to dry under a leaf. We, of the numerous, poisoned and out of work. A city of people full of antidepressants. You say at least the tyrant was pure in his hate, not bumbling, weak, or ineffectual. What is it the earth wants us to do? A nursery rhyme is what the sick child might recite to herself. Is it up to us to see she learns the verses? Silver dollar, the sky patch is polished, translucent as skin. The heart begs. Can we light the world for others? In the novel, a brother dies alone, simple and half-mad, wearing the old men's clothes he's found in thrift stores. The sister has been called, but she cannot come. In the pain shop, in the off-lift, never a case, the loss of beauty. *Oh let's not hurt him, oh let's not hurt her, let's simply make them disappear,* say the lovers about the lovers they are about to betray.

Grace Period

The days were a flame. You threw the blanket down. The days smoldered and did not gleam. Oh, I know I should answer your late-night calls. But why do you trouble me now in my old age? The creeks, the stones, are moving out of sight. Staggering their thinking as the grasses do. I put you aside as if you were one of my dead. You had become, *en masse*, the inevitable. The cherry tree you loved out the window is now bare. Small bird in a giant's gray tresses. We know nothing of how this world is made. The doe, for instance, I saw roadside, blinking its last into the dark. I was not your last lover. You are not mine. The territory between us: nothing will perhaps grow there for years. Why not let the winds sweep in and round the stones? So that we could offer each other this: the lightest blue like a curtain in a girl's room before she wakes. Even if one of us turns away.

The City of Many Lovers

Lunedì. Martedì. Mercoledì. It's moon-day. Moon that strikes on the downbeat. Tomorrow, a day for Mars. And a day in the middle, which is a miracle. We visit your ex-lovers. Which is to say, the understanding that you could leave me tomorrow. Not the most loved. The most new. What to count on? In the Japanese film, the Buddhist praises her god in each of his 36,000 manifestations. Of course, you like me. I am round. I have no edges. You can play with me. So can your dog. Then I crawl into an absence I have been remodeling all my life—a crockery, walls smoothed with warm water. Moon Dreaming of her Brother Bronze. Cold Milk Moon over Lake and Fog Diptych. We have been here a month. I have left my people behind and adopted yours. I imagine I have made this happen. I imagine a tree falling and the tree falls. It seems both gift and penalty that I was left alone as a child. While you, in your city, learned civility.

The Harbor

You try to imagine, amidst the yellow smoke, the uniforms, the boots, the heavy boots, the all of apples. When you learned to recognize the various ferns. They grew out of the sky-turned bottom of the fallen tree. The upper world, a French wine lifted in its polished glass. You use the word polish and you notice others use it, too, because the same sky is wearing thin above them. In an abandoned cabin at the harbor, you find the photograph of yourself as a child, your cat's eye glasses the same as your three sisters'. So much better if your parents had stopped at two. Which two? You walk, or rather, try to walk, first this way, then that. A grotesquery, how the vine maples fling themselves across the path, naked, leafless as sex. The light rains down, the selflessness of light. So much you gave up when you left here, in order to leave here. What was the poem? The husband returns, in a taxi, distracted and badly spent. The wife reminds herself that there are people and cities he traveled through before they met, all the beautiful people and cities between them.

The People We Once Were

are small, spotted as pets. Closed like a door in its jam after the child has gone to sleep. Wings of butterflies at rest. All divine gestures, holding their heat. We are getting old. I can see it in the way we title rather than name things. Silver Cloud Suspended in the Wedding Ring of Sky. Full Moon the Color of Batter. The streets seem quieter, close to the reindeer and quail, those solitaries who live out certain distances. We have a candle burning. It is half past six and still dark. Soon, we will open the curtains. From where does the premonition of death come? In the book of famous photographs, the woman with cancer stares out, fierce and shorn on her trip to Egypt. Who will be able to render us with such love? The child at five says good-bye forever to her twin brother. The ten-year-old girl steps between her father and her mother. With silvered breath, we turn a corner, and there they are. Granddaughter. Older sister. First lover. Best friend.

The Aqua Robe

How impressionable the skin is. I sleep in my thickly embroidered robe. I brocade you. The eye of the fold is the place where the knee meets the fabric. Designers say it determines everything. *Even if a curtain does not rise or part but only surrounds the action.* . . . To reach this morning's calm, I have had to enter from the side. I have had to disappear into my own distances. Blue shroud, I am wrapped in my luck, soft stripe between violet and green. I know my value. It is in singleness. When I'm in a nursing home, you say, will you come and have sex with me, even if I can't remember your name. We are in the time of year ruled by the moon, the changing emotions of water. The woman who uses her life completely throws it into the tide. A very rare specimen, the aqua flower of limestone columbine. Underwing of a slope covered with common forget-me-not.

Still Green

Buy the deep blue cloth and wrap it round the alder. The yellow warblers will fall, floor by floor, through the leaves. Sit on the leather couch until it is soft enough for guests. Here, high in the mountains, where the world began. The yard is torn up, the graves disturbed, penstemon and ruffled columbine gone. Go out with your broom, the limbs heavy with early snow. Touch the shoulders of your subjects and let them rise. You're getting sweet on each other, so perhaps that is where the hours go, into the making of pink and orange jams. You could spread your work out across a wood table for days. You could give each other this spread. The rest comes easy—cranberries and winter squash, the raking of stones from the field. Imagine your hair, a prayer bundle of straw. Ask where are you going and with whom. Time has stopped rolling and is teetering, silver gold, on edge. A day of shearing rain, pouring sun. Many have left, but today, as far as you know, no one is leaving. Call them. Let them hear your voice, soft from its cave, so soft the answering machine cuts it off.

III.

How can we show, without betraying them, those simple things sketched between the twilight and the sky? By the virtue of stubborn life, in the circle of artist Time, between death and beauty.

— René Char

Art of the Pacific Northwest

1.

Sea green, black, topaz, and crystal brushed onto the carved cheekbones of the moon in her four phases. The one that brings the fragrances, laced and murmuring, like a Persian script. The one stirring the pollen that impregnates the great cedars. The one too intoxicated to make it up her own stairs. You smile, expecting to meet your own mother or grandmother, and when you don't, you feel disoriented, almost defiled. A Skykomish woman weaves a blanket in the traditional way, reviving a method that has almost become extinct. Gathering the tufts from the mountain costs her six months. Weaving the goat hair into strands, another six. Inside the earth-and-sky pattern, what does my people mean? Here is a tribe of yellows, a tribe of blues. Troop meaning one soldier, or a group of soldiers. The blanket is heavy; only the eldest may try it on, though "it feels like heaven," one of them is quoted as saying.

2.

In her studio, a graphic artist constructs her own model town, paints with resins the tiny buildings she bought on eBay: Starbucks. Home Depot. Walmart. A town she plans to blow up. To set on fire. Cool breeze on the outer deck. Her father's abstract paintings on the walls. Bathroom tiles a shade called wasabi. In the handbook of revelations, one learns of each creature's desire and the pain that is caused by its privation. She serves us couscous and raw oysters. We open two bottles of good wine. My people, blind practitioners of loss. The bald eagle squats. The salmon rises. The sun dances on the water in its glass hut. Even the cloud has a turn to speak, as well as the candle. The artist, prey to melancholy, prepares for it, saying that in the hour of our deaths, may we remember what we have taken.

The Butterfly Conservatory

The colored lights they are always stringing. The placemats they set. How I stay past an initial shyness at my own delight. A Large White dies, bodiless, a papyrus with fading ink. Nothing dies with less evidence of rot. When the scrolls were found at Qumran, there were forty copies of the Psalms. Eight lines in each stanza, read from right to left. What it must have felt like to recognize one had discovered this famous text, perhaps in its original form. They carry their prayer books, their portable shrines, the ones that depict their battles with the wind. A written language has trapdoors to fall through. When I talk to myself, they open, too. A butterfly suddenly becomes impatient in its shroud, the one that resembles a gray leaf. The one imitating a raindrop. Could any of us mark the moment we realized we were unhappy? Could we mark the moment we wanted out? In the house of the butterflies, there is a glass case. In it, hundreds of pupae. Monarchs strung like jade earrings along the wire threads. Painted Ladies like drying seaweed or straw. *Please, don't let me hurt anyone today.* Who will make me to lie down in green pastures. Who will prepare a table before me.

The Card of Atmosphere

You feed your brother, damaged beyond repair, apples, dried bananas, baked things, doling them out so he doesn't choke, singing to him of widgeons and pigeons. The bargirls in leather, the tattooed butches—your two friends, one with cancer, who took their lives. And the men who are not butterflies, tramping the soil, who have called the sun down, melted the ice caps. I see them as other and you see them as twins. How far the distant shores of the heart. Your tears for them like the light on the willow after rain. Like a shop of glass beads on the Rialto. For a month, we have walked arm in arm in the park. Sweet our mouths, the lake ribboned with pearl. I tell you that I abandoned my own beloved grandmother to thieves, that because I would not care for her, she lost her home. I had a lover who had to tear at me to get free. You craft the exquisite language of your weeping now, as if for me. Something I might place in the threshold of my workroom.

Winter Plumage

You read from the Japanese cookbook. The recipe Wind in the Pines is named for what the boiling water sounds like. Outside, a quiet shoveling. No sound but the scrape, hitting the ice below. Winter plumage: duller for the gold finch. You have come to the end of a certain relationship with your brother. You ask me to go with you, perhaps initiate a change. You say you want to know him in a way you haven't known him. In the institution, where he sits amid the grotesque faces of the deformed at birth, all mute, all the products of a curse, his shirt is dirty and he, rocking, recedes. The kind of person we would be if we had been so abandoned. While off in the distance, the young family, still on the farm, stand waiting for you to bring them news of his speaking. *All sentient beings*, for whom the Buddhists pray. *Place in them, like the snowflakes, a sphere of light.* When the finch return in summer, their feathers will have turned a brighter gold, an arrival too much for any of us to imagine.

Reading Beckett

We gave them your mute brother. We gave them our dead. Even hired someone to kill the cat so it wouldn't suffer. By now, each one of them will have forgotten each of us. They will have become a rock-hard insight into themselves. Was there a children's ward? Was there anyone who was kind? We heard that there was a woman and that they sometimes let her hold them. *It is the mythological present, don't mind it.* There is a shambles at the edge of every town. My bone-thin uncle hit by a truck, riding his bicycle to get cigarettes, probably drunk. Born of both mortal and divine parents—how any of us must begin. What stages we are made to perform on. Born of mothers, always poor and in training. Born of fathers who inherit a foreign land. Toward what are we led? We don't know, but we feel luckier than them. And sometimes, to our shame, it makes us laugh.

Land of Lemons

How everyone must feel when the laughing stops, cars and boats looking silly, like toys, the sky full of round things—the shape of fruit. Listen. We have authored a haiku about today's date: *White and gold ribbons / flutter outside our windows / to scare away birds.* From the glass, clear and delicious. Here, the people must shout in the streets. Here, there is juice squeezed into pitchers. No one worries about the fields drying out. They just do: ochre, caramel, saffron. The sun plants its replicas in our yards. We fly in and the smoke clears. Our doom is banished outside the frame, along with helicopters spotting for wildfires. The land of onions that has been recently dug up. Barefoot and woozy through the summer duff, we walk with our bright lids half-closed. Happy-stupid, while the illness grows inside us. Sure that god won't leave us because we are ill.

The Integrity of Time

I quicken the animal out with the in of where I've been. Overheat of wood smoke. Oil from my frying. The creek iced over. Only the topcoat of snow melts. *Disgrace*, the novelist writes of desire, snarling. I realize I have talked with you about this novel before. It was before I read it. Before I met you. A kind of flecked shining off the fever dream still, like flakes of dried ginger, scales of salmon. Look, this was a house where there was much pain to come. I want to learn to love it here, be calm inside it. Outside is below zero, and I haven't yet fed the birds. I want to reestablish pain's mortality. You read to me from a book of meditations on death. The author says that because we come into the world crying, to imagine our own death should make us laugh. But not to imagine another's. If time is the movement we divide into anniversaries of gain and loss, how did we ever agree on a common measure? I drive to town, the blue darkening above the strange yellow hill. As if someone were entering a room just as someone else was waking.

The Art of Cure

There is the art of diagnosis, Ezra Pound wrote, and the art of cure, which is scribbled on thin paper, stained with the juice of blackberries, folded and refolded by a compulsive into the field, into grasses so dry they make us gasp, into peppermint leaves, vials of water. Thorns, too, and thistles for protection, and would that be worth all the time you spend alone? And what would cure be, past presumption—past asking the gods to please give back our keys, past letting the ancient tree fall? Let our deaths come. Let them come as a songbird, caught in a snare fashioned of horsehair and reeds. Not to have brought them carelessly upon each other. They say the planting of lupine, cosmos, and yarrow will call the butterflies in. Likewise, a basin filled with wet sand. Remember how you once stood at a window above a lake, exclaiming "I love it here," at the boats below and the light on water.

The City of Art and the City of Love

O Delicate, O Anxious One even the breeze disturbs, in the heat of no-sleep, in the dark that cannot be lit, duct-taped to the bed so the family can go out at night, there in that absolutely wrong hour, you worry about love. Anything could happen, though it always could. As a child, before the catastrophe, you would add the names in Greek to a guide you called The Little Flower Neck. Until it broke, you loved walking in the nearby fields. One never knows when one is just on the other side of happiness, or sadness, the day before, for instance. You open the heavy curtains and there they are, pale and loosely woven like water. Sheers, your mother called them, that drug of grace. *Breathe your breath into my book of changes.* The flowers know when it is day and not night. The flowers recognize a not-self. What will happen to your precious loneliness now? Remember that no one wants to say forever. Yet, concealed in nectaries, the honey darkens. In the created life, handed to you, handed to everyone.

Artist Time

A Japanese artist creates her sculptures out of tangled twigs and wire, then hangs a bare bulb in front of them. The sculptures form the shadows between the bulb and the wall. The sculptures are the apparatus. Ten days ago, we were driving to an airport at dawn. And here we are, as if it had never happened. The Buddhists say this is all we have: view that opens when we open our arms, fresh water lagoon, wild fennel. A woman we meet speaks of parallel time, how she found someone else's painting in a dumpster. And that is why, under her minimalist gradations of pastel sky, these marvelous nubs and intrusions. My lover, you forget: where we've been, what we've done. And yet, you have lost nothing. In the moment you chose the apple, the rustic blue bowl. In the moment you chose me, over and over.

IV.

The Nine Senses

See how the morning light lies on the top planes of the venetian blinds. And the tree, whole and shining, in the spaces between. Through the cracks, look. A simile, its little hinge. Today's story. The hour's lesson. Pinstripes on the bed, dimming as the roomy world darkens. The Sufis say the five senses are supplemented by four more. Curl of the living creek under the squabbling of birds, their breakfast talk, their famous comebacks. Taste of one's tongue until there is coffee. Perhaps the extra four senses contribute to our sense of the *surreal*, as resolution of the real and the dream. How the pen must leave the page, in a flourish, to cross its bridges. The slight push of will required to close one's eyes. To rest and let the found be found. Mother I reach out to with knitted brow, or to the side when I want my sister. I have called you so I can hear your voice and see light falling at the same time. Cob of dried corn under the bird feeder. Cob of mullein flower. Cob of the gums.

Clairvoyance (Sunlight)

Sunlight falls through the square window into the water of the inside pool and is reflected onto the blue wall above it. Ghost-handkerchiefs, whiter at the folds. When I make a wave with my hand, they disperse, as in a blizzard, but soon, the fluttering squares return. I could say that when I'm gone, I'll come back to you like this, talking to myself the way the soul does. If that is true, then whose soul is this? Sometimes I can sense death coming, and it is white, too. A name that enters, disturbs the field as the first butterfly might. Mourning Cloak with its velvet tippet, its golden hem. There are the two-by-fours that hit us in the sensory world. And the medium approach of evening, shuffling the pines. There is the differentiation of colors, louder for the painters. When I wake at dawn with a low-grade fever of the mind and go out on my porch to cool it off, the spider web I don't see until rain strings its beads. Or the dead, who wear the softer hands of the living.

The Book of Spells

Here, quiet as stone. A solid that blocks the ears. In our little camp, sparkling with mica. In the water, which is the color of the stones. A local artist tells us that he begins every scene with an underpainting of lavender and violet—I love you, I love you, said silently to oneself, in order that it not turn to something bad. The sky clouds, a lake slowly freezing into sheen, the force of a new condition moving above it. Why I am so fascinated by the painters: they leave behind a collection of loose prayers. I read, in the book of spells, that there are four steps to dispersing fear: to name it, to place it, to breathe into that place. The next step is where to go from there. Mouth of water chewing the world to soft, spitting the hard pebbles of shale and slate and shadow. The wind, a mix of linen and salt. Even here, inland, we hear it sifting.

Telekinesis

Over there, someone is buying a velvet scarf, pronouncing the words *willow, dream.* Over here, the buds are still sleeping. White sash around the blue waist of earth, glitter-water of the lake we have come to see. (How *beautiful,* a student says to the visitor named Green after the unseasonably dry and brown winter.) Phalanx after phalanx, the snow geese rise from the lake's sheen, then disappear as they land upon its surface. Shadows under the hills each proclaiming, I am hill. Relax. The land will greet each of us. The head will lift only so high. I am worried for my friends, who do not seem as happy as me. Their symptoms I can feel in the distance. One stood in my yard long past the time I had gone to bed, looking at the stars, which made him dizzy. *The sky is further away than you think, is it not, mama?* the son asks near the end of Beckett's novel, and the mother answers, devastatingly, no. *It is precisely as far away as it appears to be.*

The Dream Horse

after a painting by Jaune Quick-to-See Smith

When the horse was young, when its head was smooth. A lilac bowed down with spring rains. Bent from the neck, bent at the knee, facing east, pawing at a prayer carpet of mud and straw. Pawing the ground like the dog does for the buried bone. Yeats wrote that there is waking and there is dreaming, both perpetual exchange, and then there is sleep, which most resembles death, completely light or completely dark, *according to our liking*. Yet here we are, most of us, back again. Womb-wet and loosening like leaves from their buds. Horse emerging from the water-colors of dawn. As if there'd be pasture and sun shining between the rain clouds of May, parents at ballparks watching their sons and daughters play, as if there'd be fast pitch forever. Oh, Irreparable. Aquifer cracked so deeply and extensively underneath the world's mines. The earth can never be what it once was.

Clairvoyance (Your Word)

Your word is *echo*, mine is *unfold*. My lover has picked the word *pool*. We have let a cool room, walking distance to the shore. We have each left a known paradise for an unknown. You unfold slowly my gift from its box. Cut-velvet, the color of merlot. But time unfolds is not unfolded—unless one says by whom. Some butterflies flail so wildly they rip from their shroud. Some pelicans land so clumsily they break their wings. We sit at the pebbled beach, picking through the precious stones—what is it that will change my guests and me? What word, what jade, what carnelian? The pelicans sail with brakes on over the waves, the slowest gliding we have ever seen. The ocean, with its huge shoulders, moves its furniture across the floor. Our mouths are not wide enough to make that sound. We unfold our small words, one by one, against rock walls. Only pool echoes.

Red Moon

If there are only three senses that allow time to pass, which one will stop it at the checkpoint? Which one will allow it, as in a game of cards, to skip its turn without wagering a bet? We are offered an album of temporary tattoos. We choose the snake that doesn't bare its fangs. We chose the word *warming*, in itself a safe word, so that we don't have to use the word *threat*. Which is incandescent this evening, yellow as a sulphur's wing. The flicker of a living creek through foliage. A red moon, black, singed from the fires. The multiple tidings of a red moon. We have outlived our ideas and our schedules for the next books. We have fantasized about collaboration. We have arranged the feathers of our mothers and our fathers in what we thought was the best possible combination. Yet, when the farmer goes to his garden in the pre-dark, close to ten, the earth in his hand is still hot.

Telepathy

1.

You reject the idea that language and thought are one. Language part of the old "folk psychology." Hermetic or hermeneutic—the girl in the jaunty cap, dressed in stripes, talking to the fish that stands in her cup? *Hey, I see the calf you are, in the dry lands, on your favorite walk to the pond. High above the small dreary town, where your brother, who does not speak, rocks back and forth on his haunches.* Everyone, an article in the magazine says, has had her heart broken at least once. Speak to that—wind, hurtful on your face, sky, jawbone of the mountains. Boulders as big as cows. You recognize the one who wishes as the one who interferes, whose desires masquerade as revelations. You assume everyone has something to say, even if you don't understand it. Out of range: what spills to the sides of the straight-ahead question, answers fished up like a ring from the drain, hair and grit impossibly tangled. You live, listening for shuffling in the cupboards.

2.

The corpus callosum—shimmering web—allows the two hemi-
spheres to speak to each other. Like fire and its shadow. The
metaphysics of spark. In this way, he might feel your need to come
closer. One hears or overhears, which is a puzzle to be undressed. It
turns out, into the open. "What do you want to ask your brother,"
I say, closing my eyes. "Love," you say. I say, "That's not a question."
They taught me to feel with my mind across to their own, a woman
writes of her childhood with the Egyptians. To sense is not to will,
but to perceive. Spring morning. We stand in the lavender dark of
first light, the mute striking like moths against our knees—trees,
distance, premonition. Talk with the winds. You have never done
that before, overwhelmed by the extent of the invisible. For instance,
a friend calls to whisper that she has suddenly lost her voice. She
fears something is terribly wrong, in that she has lost it. I write her
words on paper and place them in a small tin, then bury it within
me so she can find them.

Yellow Warblers

They are birds meant for willow, camouflaged midair. Where all is suddenly yellow warbler. New thoughts flit through a nation, promising repair, and absolve us of our responsibility for the weather. Sparkling tent of leaves we live under. The tent is big and you can still sit up in it, reading about birds while birds wash up dead on shore. When they asked you about the aqua robe, you pointed to the sky. When you were young, you wanted to escape your mother. So you chose your famous lesbian name and the best Mexican papayas at the market. We didn't know that bell would toll so soon. Torn between the guides who lead us and those whose very being plumps the heart—our twins, our lovers. The spellings of angle and angel are often confused. You are setting it up so all of them can circle around the house. Act the species you will become in a different season.

Clairvoyance (Moon)

Moon has names for all her girls: Angel, Darling, Novia. Trees are pollen merchants when green, the holy color, is at its apex. There are baby rabbits in the night gardens, eating the world down. There are scooters to ride after dinner. There are presents to be wrapped in the thinnest, potable, yellow threads of light. Always, there are books to cry over. Someone stays up until dawn, when he smokes his cigarettes on the threshold. Someone walks to the edge of her village, as appearance goes to work on the dark. What we remember of earth: the rain-washed centers. So that we must have at one time seen them as panes of glass. If there are three things that proceed from our seeing—beauty, love, and sadness—perhaps it is sadness that casts its shadow between the other two. There are the heart people, the ones we know as children. There are the familiars, who are here to counter despair. There are companions we recognize as a danger to us—and they might be us. It's curtains for you, we say, closing them.

Lazuli Bunting

There is the obvious: slow down. Though the river water fledges, though the grasses plume overnight, though the bird-green cloud of pollen from the pine tree flies. Lilac at the center. Activate, whispered to the home. I am not scared of you. I am delighted by you. What could come between us? To the east, the drawing down of morning, to the west, you on the phone, your liking-yourself voice, your charm and complaint. The tipsy, flirting, cheap-date sway of dandelions. Yes, we stand too close to death. We are marked when we do. I hate that we were holding each other when it hit the glass. *Its neck, its lovely azure neck.* Sometimes when I am up here alone for days, it's as if I have no family, no lover, no friends. Which one of us will last longer, fluttering above the other? They say the angels are provided with two, three, or four wings. The mute withhold their secrets, as do the blind. Or those struck mute, struck blind.

Teleportation

I was splitting wood, the moisture seeping from the split, the metal so dumb and the nuthatch who, when I paused, landed next to the ax. You will bring your troops like this, your unquiet into my quiet. My stoop. My stomping grounds. You are the bird who doesn't belong. Three notes, a trill. You are not here yet, in person, and so may never be. Or say the snow geese are in Baja or the grain fields near Sacramento. Vibrating, trembling in their resistance to come back. Or say I want to, from here, feel that I am there. We all already know how to be ghosts, how to slip in the door without making the Buddhist bell ring, how to dash our hands in someone else's dish water. There, the bowl of bright eggs, the quiche on the counter, the blackbirds playing slots and cashing in. The dead do this easily, passing, disinterested, into our lives, where we kneel, pulling cheat grass from the garden beds. Never worrying if they are in the right place. Do you?

Blue Fruit

Juniper, heavy-seeded as if with pearls. The meadow as the crescent moon sets. How together we once picked Italian plums. Once, by a mountain lake, the trees wore ribbons round their waists. We walked with our arms spread to each side. When we were closed in by snow, we parked facing the river. The yellow hills blurred in the froth of falling light. In the draws, the abandoned campsites of summer. What now, whispered between each phrase. Do you remember in the Chinese movie how the peasants rose when they heard the wind, how they unbent from planting rice in the paddies? They closed their eyes, let wind take their sleeves. Think of the underside of the birch leaf disclosing itself. How blue the shadow fruit of green.

Clairvoyance (Little Evening)

Little evening, I walk across the stone bridge, helloing the river, without thinking, uncertain whether I have said anything aloud. All it has shown me is its surface. The old mill is cerise. The sound of traffic is from the village. The berry bushes drop their scarlet seeds. May I never get used to them applauding my arrivals. I have learned to love the body—loose sacs of my buttocks, papery skin underneath my breasts. I have stood on the edge and looked in. I saw a woman without visible ties to children. I saw a womb, pink with shop rags across its floor. One of the steps of initiation for the shaman was to imagine herself a skeleton, all bone. When she returned, the emptiness was with her. If it is true that birds fly with the sound of the Atlantic in one ear and the sound of the Pacific in the other, it might be impossible to stray off course. If, on the bridge, I step aside for the stranger, who says, "I agree that our river is beautiful."

V.

You who followed the absent fortune
of pilgrims, come back to your friend
rooted here, sealed
in harm's garden of jars.
— *Christopher Howell*

Trouble

It's three times as big as normal. It's a lesion, a soiled sheet. It is tired, stuffed with cotton, like a pillow. Standing at the counter, shoveling food inside its mouth, staring straight ahead, like a cow. Do we really have no guide here? Something has gone wrong. The source of illness like the source of a river. The introduction of a foreign object of ill will. It smokes. It reeks. It gets too riled up. The beginning of it, not necessarily in order. The spirit is fickle and will abandon you like a flock, a sesquipedalian wave of wings on the horizon. The altars you have built, to the dead, in front of ferns, will, in the end, be just a body to the doctors. Even if you perfume it; even if you pray. There are hours you won't be able to account for. You will disappear, heatedly. The rooms will be cold. They will make you sick before they make you well.

The Symposium on Sleep

No one mentions women in the Symposium on Sleep. The bodies flash all night like solar flares. What a candle might feel like, softening, burning from its center. A slash pile set with crumpled newspapers between its limbs, doused with kerosene, then lit. That quick: the Iraqi man at the open market, selling sugar at half price, takes his last breath and pulls the pin. Sugar substitute for what? We are left with no continuum, having been untethered from the moon, her light cracked like wing bones between his teeth. Digging for the marrow that would calm us. Then what? Choose *all* the words. Though sometimes you will be swept up like a leaf. I rub lavender oil into the scar on my friend's breast, tiny, given the size of the tumor. The longer, horizontal gash. What alliances do we make now? The wild comes back and the rains in shambles, an old way of being on earth that included finding our bearings. Go out, the voice says. There is still something for you to see. So awake. So ready to be fed.

Orient

Say you have seen inside your body. Your organs have hit the light of day, a film that couldn't be more out of focus. Say you are ashamed of what you see and what is growing inside you, sore and orange as a nectarine. Sometimes it is a matter of one small thing, a gift to send away with a friend. Or to take the morning slow, making calls the way the birds do, to know the others are all safe, in their places. September's sister-quiet, when there is no complaint and you don't speak ill of anyone. Pressed between the days, which are close as reeds. You are used to being in control of your life. You have been lucky is another way of putting this. You try to imagine what it might feel like to think without language. You look at your mother, staggering with her deep heart, or those women who are nine-tenths the needs of others, and you wonder if language has shrunken you. To a body with a foreign language of its own.

The Operation

Remember that there are guardians reserved only for you: night, mist, blue sky, the east, pine boughs in heat, the sexual organs of women, ghosts, graves, the bones, hair and teeth of the deer, and so on. The body you have never named, though you are known by it. You can feel it now, clawing like a small mammal at your groin, a word that is embarrassing, close to groan and loin. Located. A cushion full of pins. A list of all the places you haven't told. During the ceremonial dismemberment of the body, you read, a Siberian shaman's heart, liver, and kidneys are replaced with chunks of quartz. She is stuffed with solidified light. Your own mortality? Bruised and thick. Who will see it when they open you up? Favor your left leg, tuck the other inside you like a heron. It is said that you will go through the clouds. You will go through the place where the Doctors go. Be quick. You must be back before they sew you up.

Wood Getting

The wound closes behind you, deep with black speckled rocks. The return is all surface silver. Your reproductive life, stored in the secret vault. The moment your boots suddenly fill. When you were young, you cut wood on the near side of the creek. You didn't cross it, log by log, alone. A door opened or there was no door. Why bother about the ones that did not exist for you? The passage between life and death—it must be dangerous and long. For the Persians, the color of heaven was green. You look down so you don't slip, where you encounter the sky. At four, a visible dousing of its lamps. Only once did you see a fish, twenty years ago, when you built the bridge. That bridge has now tipped to its side. And your friends who helped build it? One is dead. One is lost. The rest leave you to this soul-work on the bank.

Benign

The book, into its second printing, is entitled Amongst Old People: A Dream. Who helped and didn't help is not important. You came through to the flower-shelves. For months, you fought the fog. Why not believe in the good until it disproves itself? Today, it comes with brightness and frost melting off the roof. It makes you toast and drips the berry syrup on it. Ah, your friends, their fingertips, a red leaf pinned to the door. So that now you are tied to the sun and wind, however marginally. The range of images in your theater—what are they? When will they let up? You see now the dirty films that you allowed. A new emptiness is sewn inside you. You have walked the bridge of knives. You have unbuttoned your coat so you could twirl. These are the variations: your lover will call you the Bird with No Excuses. The wind will think you, too, are the wind.

Recuperation

That I am taken back, given back, that is, we are all on loan. Arboreal forest, I reaffirm my vows to you, my anthropomorphic costume. I came late to the village. The moon was a lopsided egg an angel might brood over. Appearing in a new place under scarves. The young man who drove me spoke of the possibility of a sacred life not tied to the market economy. All the little organs of hope stacked in a pile along the road, chunked and balanced there, everyone watching for the solid ones to pick up. I have an affinity for health. Things turn out well. Why should I always be the favorite. If doctors look far enough, they can always find something wrong, so many hard lives in the distance. Blood-smell, like tramping through mud. Scooping us, no, it, the animal body, clean. Each one of us a candidate for the slaughter. Recuperate, for what? *Grandmothers*, the author wrote, a word she uses for all the unattributable sources.

Revision

But if your sphere was small, say, and you had a quarter lifetime to get it right, and you took this part out and placed it next to that, the river at night, say, black with car lights, the river at day, the murky color of your first monochromatic paintings. You have never stood in the same river twice, the professor is fond of repeating, but the woman who remembers says yes you have. Wordsworth recollecting, in captivity, the news in *nous*, or the even repetition of or's. It was All Soul's Day. I remember that I cried, though I often want visitors to go away. Yes, exactly like a river, the path irritating with traffic on the right but my eye to the left, on the whiteness. The way a river will speed, the way it will eventually leave the road to the back road where the rich, in woolens, drive tractors. Nothing has ever come to me unrevisable. It comes at me, *as is*, a button missing. I went downstairs as usual but they met me halfway. The earth with its cars and leaves and roofs seems to take up most of the window.

The Return, or Dreaming Back

In the fig or the "hermetically sealed" half oranges the young artist stuffs into a burlap bag, I see my little lost organ everywhere. I want to forgive it. The way it demanded soul-participation in my life. Its overtaking, as often the mad do. As you did. Ending here, in this studio above the bridge. We are in a dark time. We can feel it. We cannot meet in the house we used to share. I cannot know you as once I knew you. Master and slave. Mother and Child. We have exhausted all manner of kin. Soon after they were married, Yeats' wife began to talk in a trance, channeling the crabby old root-men of the dead. They said her past would rewind like film on a spool until her ties to the passionate body thinned. A light snow falls. It falls into the river. A weighting of the sand on either side. Be gone, my disease. To your own tough luck. Only then can I be spirit and not be called more simply dead. Only then can I rightly be born again.

VI.

The Empty Inn

In my childhood, I would have called these walls plum, then perhaps claret. Plush and horsehair of Victoriana. A well-appointed inn that smells of rats. In the back of which the moss-girl sleeps alone, rises alone, dresses in the silks and satins she has come to favor underneath her wool, now that she has grown. Her face still and round as the lake. She sits in the abandoned restaurant, knitting and unraveling a scarf, unable to choose between two almost identical greens. What color would I call those walls now? Ten years ago, or maybe yesterday, she left the beds to their chenille. The half-used bags of flour, the grill left unclean, the flies that hatch and seed the floors and sills. *Imagination, my child.* Surround yourself with the good as if you had a child growing inside you: wool and lakes and wild apples. Find a corner to accumulate in, like the snow. As if any minute the owner will make his way back again.

The Watchful Child

My first name came out of a book or a cloud or a sound pleasant to my mother's ears. The second is my father's and doesn't suit me. The third ties me to the dead, is folded in their cloth. People of the cloth, aren't we all so? My fourth name is translated. Here, the leaves block the road. Our names change, but with sidebars, the way we like them. (The barter-work later will come.) What is a raddled moon? Reddened. What is a ribbon bird? Eye shadow. Namesake: to dress up the little girls like the sky. Which is glossed with distance, twilight, blue flax. Which is objective, removed, and often directionless. Like many people today, I've spent the day in a car, exchanging money for dubious goods and services. Don't you think, if you were dying, you wouldn't do that? I keep talking to my names, asking how best to serve them. As I have begun talking to everything.

The Angel Applicant

title from a painting by Paul Klee

White umbel of dogwood, blue flax that closes in the heat—
I say them to ward off the suffering of my father. Who taught me
complaint, who was never grateful. We drink champagne with
bitters. Your father called you jewel. This evening, the sky changed
every few minutes: rain, then dark, then silver. What I mean is
that no one blames the sky. I have kept my past close, a quiet
between friends, asking: *How are you? Do you feel loved enough?*
Always ready to applaud deviation. The birthday chain of events.
The hopscotch grid of chalked dangers. Daughters in rows, in the
pulpits, like the furred antennae of moths. Don't you have that,
too? Don't you, my brethren? The sky unfolds in perpetuity. The
earth is rose-dipped, red green. If I close my eyes, it will soon be
over, I learned in the family, in the factory.

Thin as a Rail

Everyone taken care of this morning, everyone tender and lost. The lonely boy down the road who flirted with men is now a frail adult. Though his rickety pride still surfaces, stirred by the sight of the creek where he grew up, the flagstones he laid with his brother. If I look for him, he's everywhere, too fat, or else rail-thin like the shorebird whose body is so compressed it can hide among the dense grass and reeds. In May, I was burning with fever. In June, I had the spells. Why we are always ready to accept the worst: because we want to take it in and care for it, too. The man in the courtroom, after his daughter's murderer admits guilt, goes berserk, lunging and punching, trying to kill him. All day, the television replays this. What is important to say to one another? *This is what happened to me. I was a child and did not speak. In the end, I was too much for everyone.*

De Profundis

Holy brothers, your dark leprosy is echoed in the sparrow-flecked fields of late November. Moleskin of the hillside. Yellowed velvet of the lawns. And the mill-stream, which I borrow from the poet Trakl. There are those of you, like him, who threw yourselves in front of stallions as children. There are those of you born into serial pain. There are those who run from the room where something unspeakable has occurred. Into the woods where the traitors' bodies hang. Visions of the presidency: our mad renditions. Why him and not me? Why me and not you? The have-a-heart traps we can't seem to enlarge. How to sing you back, wounded soldiers, to the power and dread of earth, which is divided into the hidden and the revealed. *There is a light that fails in my mouth,* Trakl wrote. It is a poetry that does not seek to rise. Oh, mother who bears the child in the white moon of ruin. A string of blue globes shining down his spine.

Inventing a People Who Are Lacking

If I could think of the earth this morning as coffee-stained, but bright of leaf where there is hay and fern, subtle and boyish in its reserve—not me, but close to me—then perhaps I could be more compassionate toward men. Surely the earth is genderless. Like the kitten I found, hermaphrodite, its balls not yet dropped, its back rough and lined with summer felt. There is a mountain above me, which I have learned to call the sky. What it would mean to begin talking into its image. That it is not too late, that we are here, and charged with helping? *The artist, closer to the autistic, the schizoid, the infant, in her oceanic connectedness to the world, is not "patient" but "doctor"—if we follow Deleuze.* The world with its endless set of symptoms. Like a full moon, its plaster punched in. When I came upon the old cemetery, its tablets thin, I sank perceptively into it and that seemed wrong. We have lost the ones who weep, the lonely ones, who are on the other side. So far from home they might forget they have one.

Talk to the Golden Birches

Emissaries, but of what? Peppered with mold and myrrh, clawed like cloud-strips, they grow in the copse on the hill. The first one I find, lying on its side, the next half-covered with moss. Gilt, adjective, their colors of gold. Gilt, laid on the surface. Gilt, *young female swine*. There is a surprise in every forest. There are many etymologies to cross, and directions, not paths, to decide on. Satyr, black mushroom, sticking its foot from the grave. Tree fungi, so stiff they won't tear off. Before the hieroglyph was deciphered, it was thought of as a language not to be read but *revealed*. One had to be initiated to understand it, to pick through the litter at its feet. To tip the cereal bowl of breakfast stars. The river is wind-pocked. The leaves brew a tea exactly the same color as the bark—metallic, tin snipped and rough. "Where did November come from?" How old is the soul? Worn out, gouged with display. *Our dear exotic companion.* Marked by public tragedy—those who locked hands and fell from the towers—and the private: those who looked away.

Talk to the Water Dipper

I heard it fall and then its shuffling in the unburned paper of the last fire. Do you have a story about a chimney and a bird? Because here I am in a forest, and it is just before dark. I was afraid to open the door. The woman who has lost her memory says that she doesn't like it here, that there is no one or no place to visit. She wishes the furniture weren't an art piece. She wishes she weren't always bored. *Is there a higher power / there is a higher power* reads the plinth of the sculpture on the path, but to me it is too simple a question / answer. In the life of the water dipper, that was probably the only time it would be inside the house of a human, which must appear like a giant trap with upper reaches. Everything must seem square and, thus, wrong. No fly throughs. No under-things and bridges. Nothing to eat either, all jar. But it must have liked the stove door that opened of its own accord to a world beyond all previous measure. What did I mean there? Not in the way it does, mimicking the stream. A myth—but that's the rub, something's got to turn into something else. A myth: the water dipper, the mossed cottage trees, the tin man, the next world, the rose, etc.

Talk to the Milkweed Pod

This is how a bird must sleep, if it sleeps at all, under a duvet of drifting pollen and recovered thread. Gray pod, just like a bird's beak, its eyes a wrinkle, a small seam, so closed that I'm not sure it has them. Pod that now startles, awakes. Inside, the walls are lined with beeswax, encaustic, smoothed out for the seeds—apostrophes signaling their possession. See how much is trimmed? Barely an inch. A spill of bangs, a pile of lash under the chair. The ditch is filled with milkweed. Wind is tugging hard. The rain is warm, a plant-warmth, an ideal. Can I join them? Can I open the trapdoor, a patch made of grass slats, with a rope—which is the wind—to hoist it? No time to be sacred. Whether I move or they do, whether I sell this house or they sell theirs. We are here with the separation in front of us. I bow to it as the milkweed do. In various stages of disarray. Shepherdess of the Inner Fields, who stirs us. Who comes, paradoxically, in the form of rest.

Talk to the Great Suffering

Get that place into your pores. Who knows when you'll ever go back again. Standing next to the crowded files of autumn grass. Marsh woven to fawn. Straw warblers. Something about that woman yesterday, burning leaves in her housedress, creating a public nuisance with the smoke, while near her yard, the forests were ankle deep in them. You have been learning to let imagination lead. Where did we go wrong is still an important question. So, too, why are we here. In the paper, this morning, the photograph of a dying bird, on a beach of the Black Sea, grimy with oil after the recent spill. Its neck stretched back, its silent open scream. Then your walk home, cold and silver. You have your gentleness. You would carry it large in your arms up to the light. You, who have turned on it as you have on thousands. What else but the world did it have to trust? It was black, a burnt corpse. It couldn't breathe so it couldn't fly. It looked unreal like a painting by Morris Graves: *Bird Maddened by the Sound of Machinery in the Air. Little-Known Bird of the Inner Eye.* Please forgive us, you remember whispering as you closed the page. As the clean-up crew worked behind it, incrementally.

Tag End

The ribbons tap like fingernails on the glass when the wind blows. I have hung new ones, from my gifts, on the crossbars. I have packaged an interior, a valley of chimes. Unlimited, is another way to put this. The days are finished and the new ones begin. Here, perhaps, a handful that have no home. If I had wings, this is how I'd fold them, my arms wrapped around you. You, then, would be my divinity. This is how it works: they, those we love, drop off the ends of the earth. Something in our aging, which approves it. Look, I have white hair and yet my parents are still here. Does that make us less committed to each other? I think of the Hopi, the Navajo, in the southwest, dancing so the deer will continue. I think, as I have thought since I was young. Bestiary. Aviary. Imaginary. We overwatch the world. How many plum seasons we have abandoned.

Grateful acknowledgment is given to the editors of the following journals in which some of the poems first appeared:

Antioch Review: "The Empty Inn"

Bellingham Review: "Talk to the Great Suffering," "Talk to the Milkweed Pod"

Boston Review: "Sparrow," "Clairvoyance (Sunlight)"

Cerise Press: "Trouble," "Orient," "The Operation," "The Return, or Dreaming Back," "Recuperation"

Columbia: A Journal of Literature and Art: "Reading Beckett," "Telekinesis"

Crazyhorse: "Clairvoyance (Your Word)," "Clairvoyance (Little Evening)"

Eleven Eleven: "The Nine Senses"

Field: "The City of Many Lovers"

Interim: "Attar," "Sweet Briar," "The Symposium on Sleep"

Kenyon Review: "At the Shore," "Winter Bouquet," "The Lights of Earth," "Woman Inside a Tree," "The Butterfly Conservatory," "Talk to the Water Dipper," "Talk to the Golden Birches"

Knockout: "Land of Lemons," "Red Moon," "The Watchful Child," "Thin as a Rail"

Many Mountains Moving: "Bamboo"

Michigan Quarterly Review: "The Language of Flowers"

NEO: "Nettle," "Still Green," "The Nightingale's Excuse," "Grace Period"

Parthenon West Review: "The Integrity of Time," "Winter Plumage"

Pleiades: "De Profundis"

Quarterly West: "Benign"

Stone's Throw: "The Aqua Robe"

The Journal: "Ophelia among the Flowers," "Wood Getting,"
   "The Dream Horse"

Tusculum Review: "The School of the Dead, the School of Roots,
   and the School of Dreams," "The Trumpet Place," "The City
   of Art and the City of Love," "Ground for a New Goddess,"
   "Revision"

Willow Springs: "Delight," "Almost Ice," "Tag End"

"The Nine Senses," which included the "Clairvoyance" poems,
"Telepathy," "Telekinesis," and "Teleportation," won the 2009 Cecil
Hemley Memorial Award from the Poetry Society of America,
for which I am grateful. I would also like to thank the National
Endowment for the Arts for a fellowship at the Vermont Studio
Center, the Wachtmeister Foundation for a fellowship at the
Virginia Center for the Creative Arts, and Hedgebrook for my
residency there.

Much love and gratitude to my farseeing and wise first readers:
Bryher Herak, Rusty Morrison, and Robert Baker.

Thank you also to Wayne Miller for his generous editing of this
manuscript.

Notes/Sources:

The italicized or quoted lines in many of the poems are either mine, attributable to the author to whom the poem is dedicated, or from the following works: "Sweetbriar": *Go inside a stone* from the poem "Stone" by Charles Simic; "Ophelia among the Flowers": *O, you must wear your rue with a difference* from *Hamlet* by William Shakespeare; "The Harbor": *the all of apples* from the poem "The Shape of the Fire" by Theodore Roethke; "The Aqua Robe": *Even if a curtain does not rise or part but only surrounds the action* from *Drapery: Classicism and Barbarism in Visual Culture* by Gen Doy; "The City of Art and the City of Love": *Breathe your breath into my book of changes* from *The Metamorphoses* by Ovid (trans. Rolfe Humphries); "The Nine Senses": the idea of surrealism as a resolution of the real and the dream is from André Breton's *Surrealist Manifesto*; "Recuperation": *Grandmothers* as a word Rebecca Solnit uses for unrecognized sources in history, from *A Field Guide to Getting Lost*; "The Empty Inn": *Imagination, my child* from the poem "Feuillets d'hypnos" by René Char; "Inventing a People Who Are Lacking": *The artist, closer to the autistic, the schizoid, the infant, in her oceanic connectedness to the world, is not "patient" but "doctor"—if we follow Deleuze* from the essay "The Art-and-Healing Oeuvre" by Bracha L. Ettinger, published in *3 x Abstraction: New Methods of Drawing by Hilma af Klint, Emma Kunz, and Agnes Martin*, edited by Catherine de Zegher and Hendel Teicher; and "Talk to the Golden Birches": "Where did November come from?" from *The Book of Questions* by Pablo Neruda (trans. William O'Daly).

Opening section epigraphs: Corbin: *Spiritual Body and Celestial Earth: From Mazdean Iran to Shiite Iran* (trans. Nancy Pearson); Char: *René Char: Selected Poems*, eds. Mary Ann Caws and Tina Jolas (trans. Mary Ann Caws and Patricia Terry); Howell: "The Wu General Writes from Far Away," *The Crime of Luck*.

Bryher Herak

Melissa Kwasny is the author of three previous books of poetry, *Reading Novalis in Montana* (Milkweed Editions, 2009), *Thistle* (Lost Horse Press, 2006), which won the Idaho Prize in 2006, and *The Archival Birds* (Bear Star Press, 2000). She is also the editor of *Toward the Open Field: Poets on the Art of Poetry 1800–1950* (Wesleyan University Press, 2004), and coeditor with M.L. Smoker of *I Go to the Ruined Place: Contemporary Poems in Defense of Global Human Rights* (Lost Horse Press, 2009). She lives in Jefferson City, Montana.

More Poetry from Milkweed Editions

To order books or for more information, contact Milkweed at (800) 520-6455 or visit our Web site (www.milkweed.org).

Fancy Beasts
Alex Lemon

The Book of Props
Wayne Miller

Reading Novalis in Montana
Melissa Kwasny

Rooms and Their Airs
Jody Gladding

Music for Landing Planes By
Éireann Lorsung

Mission

Founded as a nonprofit organization in 1979, Milkweed Editions is an independent publisher. Our mission is to identify, nurture and publish transformative literature, and build an engaged community around it.

Join Us

In addition to revenue generated by the sales of books we publish, Milkweed Editions depends on the generosity of institutions and individuals like you. In an increasingly bottom-line-driven publishing world, your support allows us to select and publish books on the basis of their literary quality and transformative potential. Please visit our Web site (www.milkweed.org) or contact us at (800) 520-6455 to learn more.

Milkweed Editions, a nonprofit publisher, gratefully acknowledges sustaining support from Amazon.com; Emilie and Henry Buchwald; the Bush Foundation; the Patrick and Aimee Butler Foundation; Timothy and Tara Clark; the Dougherty Family Foundation; Friesens; the General Mills Foundation; John and Joanne Gordon; Ellen Grace; William and Jeanne Grandy; the Jerome Foundation; the Lerner Foundation; Sanders and Tasha Marvin; the McKnight Foundation; Mid-Continent Engineering; the Minnesota State Arts Board, through an appropriation by the Minnesota State Legislature and a grant from the National Endowment for the Arts; Kelly Morrison and John Willoughby; the National Endowment for the Arts; the Navarre Corporation; Ann and Doug Ness; Jörg and Angie Pierach; the Carl and Eloise Pohlad Family Foundation; the RBC Foundation USA; the Target Foundation; the Travelers Foundation; Moira and John Turner; and Edward and Jenny Wahl.

amazon.com **jer•me** foundation **Bush Foundation**

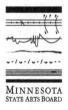

MINNESOTA
STATE ARTS BOARD

NATIONAL
ENDOWMENT
FOR THE ARTS
A great nation
deserves great art.

TARGET®

THE McKNIGHT FOUNDATION

Interior design by Connie Kuhnz
Typeset in Berstrom
by BookMobile Design and Publishing Services
Printed on acid-free 30% post consumer waste paper
by BookMobile

CPSIA information can be obtained
at www.ICGtesting.com
Printed in the USA
JSHW021241200423
40550JS00004B/12